I WILL GO WITH THEE
AND BE THY GUIDE,
IN THY MOST NEED
TO GO BY THY SIDE

EVERYMAN'S LIBRARY
POCKET POETS

DICKINSON

POEMS

EVERYMAN'S LIBRARY
POCKET POETS

Alfred A. Knopf New York London Toronto

THIS IS A BORZOI BOOK
PUBLISHED BY ALFRED A. KNOPF

Poetry is reprinted by permission of the publishers and the Trustees of
Amherst College from *The Poems of Emily Dickinson*, Thomas H. Johnson,
ed., Cambridge, Mass.: The Belknap Press of Harvard University Press,
Copyright © 1951, 1955, 1979, 1983 by the President and Fellows of
Harvard College and from *The Complete Poems of Emily Dickinson*, edited by
Thomas H. Johnson. Copyright 1929, 1935 by Martha Dickinson Bianchi;
Copyright © renewed 1957, 1963 by Mary L. Hampson: Little, Brown
and Company, Boston.

This selection by Peter Washington first published in
Everyman's Library, 1993
Copyright © 1993 by Everyman's Library

Fourteenth printing (US)

US website: www.randomhouse.com/everymans

ISBN 0-679-42907-7 (US)
1-85715-704-4 (UK)

A CIP catalogue record for this book is available from the British Library

Library of Congress Cataloging-in-Publication Data
Dickinson, Emily, 1830–1886.
[Poems. Selections]
Poems / Emily Dickinson.
p.   cm.—(Everyman's library pocket poets)
ISBN 0-679-42907-7
I. Title.   II. Series.
PS1541.A6   1993d   93-14360
811'.4—dc20   CIP

Typography by Peter B. Willberg
Typeset in the UK by AccComputing, North Barrow, Somerset
Printed and bound in Germany by GGP Media, Pössneck

EMILY DICKINSON

····················

POEMS

CONTENTS

THE POET'S ART

1 This is my letter to the World   17
2 Tell all the Truth but tell it slant   18
3 To see the Summer Sky   19
4 I would not paint – a picture   20
5 This was a Poet – It is That   22
6 She dealt her pretty words like Blades   23
7 To pile like Thunder to its close   24
8 The Martyr Poets – did not tell   25
9 I reckon – when I count at all   26
10 The Poets light but Lamps   27
11 The butterfly obtains   28
12 We – Bee and I – live by the quaffing   29
13 A word is dead   30
14 A Word dropped careless on a Page   31
15 Could mortal lip divine   32
16 Speech is one symptom of Affection   33
17 To tell the Beauty would decrease   34
18 Those fair – fictitious People   35
19 Surgeons must be very careful   37
20 Make me a picture of the sun   38
21 Delight – becomes pictorial   39
22 Your thoughts don't have words every day   ..   40
23 I dwell in Possibility   41
24 Me from Myself – to banish   42

25 It troubled me as once I was   43
26 He found my Being – set it up   44
27 I started Early – Took my Dog   45
28 Unto my Books – so good to turn   47
29 Afraid! Of whom am I afraid?   48
30 It would have starved a Gnat   49
31 They shut me up in Prose   50
32 Don't put up my Thread and Needle   51
33 They called me to the Window   52
34 I cannot live with You   53
35 She dwelleth in the Ground   56
36 To be alive – is Power   57
37 Each Life Converges to some Centre   58
38 I tie my Hat – I crease my Shawl   59
39 Pain – has an Element of Blank   61
40 A nearness to Tremendousness   62
41 'Twas such a little – little boat   63
42 The nearest Dream recedes – unrealized   64
43 All the letters I can write   65
44 Struck was I, not yet by Lightning   66
45 Again – his voice is at the door   68

THE WORKS OF LOVE

46 Who occupies this House?   73
47 Drab Habitation of Whom?   75
48 There is a solitude of space   76
49 A little Snow was here and there   77

50 Abraham to kill him 78
51 What we see we know somewhat 79
52 The Drop, that wrestles in the Sea 80
53 All overgrown by cunning moss.. 81
54 I should not dare to leave my friend 82
55 A little East of Jordan 83
56 When I was small, a Woman died 84
57 A long – long Sleep – A famous – Sleep 85
58 We talked as Girls do 86
59 The Sweets of Pillage, can be known 87
60 A Prison gets to be a friend 88
61 Her final Summer was it 90
62 I Years had been from Home 91
63 Papa above!.. 93
64 She sights a Bird – she chuckles 94
65 A little Dog that wags his tail 95
66 Civilization – spurns – the Leopard! 96
67 Within my Garden, rides a Bird 97
68 A Rat surrendered here 98
69 The Rat is the concisest Tenant 99
70 As the Starved Maelstrom laps the Navies .. 100
71 The Judge is like the Owl 101
72 One of the ones that Midas touched 102
73 A Bird came down the Walk 104
74 The Robin for the Crumb 105
75 Upon his Saddle sprung a Bird 106
76 To hear an Oriole sing 107

77 The Birds begun at Four o'clock 108
78 At Half past Three, a single Bird 110
79 She staked her Feathers – Gained an Arc 111
80 One Joy of so much anguish 112
81 The Bird her punctual music brings 113
82 Most she touched me by her muteness 114
83 A prompt – executive Bird is the Jay   115
84 No Brigadier throughout the year   116
85 An Antiquated Tree 117
86 Bee! I'm expecting you!   118
87 The Butterfly in honored Dust 119
88 The Bat is dun, with wrinkled Wings 120
89 How soft a Caterpillar steps 121
90 A winged spark doth soar about 122
91 The Spider holds a Silver Ball 123
92 A Spider sewed at Night 124
93 The Spider as an Artist   125
94 His Mansion in the Pool 126
95 I'm Nobody! Who are you? 127
96 The long sigh of the Frog   128
97 His Feet are shod with Gauze 129
98 Like Trains of Cars on Tracks of Plush   130
99 Bees are Black, with Gilt Surcingles   131
100 His little Hearse like Figure 132
101 A feather from the Whippoorwill 133
102 These are the Nights that Beetles love 134
103 Bring me the sunset in a cup 135

104 Conjecturing a Climate.. 136
105 From Cocoon forth a Butterfly 137
106 "Nature" is what we see 139
107 The Sun kept stooping – stooping – low! 140
108 The Murmur of a Bee 141
109 Some things that fly there be 142
110 If I should cease to bring a Rose 143
111 A little Madness in the Spring 144
112 A Moth the hue of this 145
113 March is the Month of Expectation 146
114 How lonesome the Wind must feel Nights .. 147
115 It was a quiet seeming Day 148
116 Summer has two Beginnings 149
117 The Gentian has a parched Corolla 150
118 A chilly Peace infests the Grass 151
119 Summer begins to have the look 152
120 With sweetness unabated 153
121 The farthest Thunder that I heard 154
122 A Wind that rose 155
123 Like Brooms of Steel 156
124 To interrupt His Yellow Plan 157
125 It makes no difference abroad 158
126 So much Summer 159
127 The Trees like Tassels – hit – and swung 160
128 These the days when Birds come back 162
129 Flowers – Well – if anybody 163
130 A slash of Blue 164

131 A Burdock – clawed my Gown 165
132 I dreaded that first Robin, so 166
133 I had no time to Hate 168
134 Love – thou art high 169
135 Love reckons by itself – alone 170
136 Love – is that later Thing than Death 171
137 Behold this little Bane 172
138 One Sister have I in our house 173
139 I never hear the word "escape" 175
140 "Why do I love" You, Sir? 176
141 Had this one Day not been 177
142 The Love a Life can show Below 178
143 There came a Day at Summer's full 179
144 You left me – Sire – two Legacies 181
145 I cautious, scanned my little life 182
146 It ceased to hurt me, though so slow 183
147 Her sweet Weight on my Heart a Night 184
148 Drowning is not so pitiful.. 185
149 He was my host – he was my guest 186
150 Of Course – I prayed.. 187
151 My period had come for Prayer 188
152 All Circumstances are the Frame 189
153 The look of thee, what is it like 190
154 It was too late for Man 191
155 Victory comes late 192
156 The Heaven vests for Each 193
157 Just as He spoke it from his hands 194

158 The Moon upon her fluent Route 195
159 Escaping backward to perceive   196
160 Just Once! Oh least Request!   197

DEATH AND RESURRECTION

161 Because I could not stop for Death 201
162 I heard a Fly buzz – when I died 203
163 Today or this noon 204
164 That it will never come again 205
165 A throe upon the features 206
166 Departed – to the Judgment 207
167 All but Death, can be Adjusted 208
168 Death is a Dialogue between 209
169 Death is the supple Suitor   210
170 Good night, because we must 211
171 If any sink, assure that this, now standing .. 212
172 Wait till the Majesty of Death 213
173 For Death – or rather   214
174 That this should feel the need of Death   215
175 To disappear enhances 216
176 Because that you are going 217
177 'Twas my one Glory 219
178 You'll find – it when you try to die 220
179 Upon Concluded Lives 221
180 Some, too fragile for winter winds   222
181 On this long storm the Rainbow rose 223
182 I read my sentence – steadily   224

183 The Fact that Earth is Heaven 225

184 Than Heaven more remote 226

185 "Heaven" – is what I cannot reach! 227

186 What is – "Paradise".. 228

187 Paradise is of the option 229

188 Lift it – with the Feathers.. 230

189 The Road to Paradise is Plain 231

190 Their Height in Heaven comforts not 232

191 Conscious am I in my Chamber 233

192 It is an honorable Thought 234

193 If my Bark sink 235

194 This World is not Conclusion 236

195 He scanned it – staggered 237

196 Somewhere upon the general Earth 238

197 Those not live yet.. 239

198 Who abdicated Ambush 240

199 My life closed twice before its close 241

200 Forever – is composed of Nows 242

201 As if the Sea should part 243

202 The Blunder is in estimate 244

203 Exultation is the going.. 245

204 A Wife – at Daybreak I shall be 246

205 Behind Me – dips Eternity 247

206 Two Lengths has every Day 248

207 The Infinite a sudden Guest 248

THE POET'S ART

1

This is my letter to the World
That never wrote to Me –
The simple News that Nature told –
With tender Majesty

Her Message is committed
To Hands I cannot see –
For love of Her – Sweet – countrymen –
Judge tenderly – of Me

2

Tell all the Truth but tell it slant —
Success in Circuit lies
Too bright for our infirm Delight
The Truth's superb surprise

As Lightning to the Children eased
With explanation kind
The Truth must dazzle gradually
Or every man be blind —

3

To see the Summer Sky
Is Poetry, though never in a Book it lie —
True Poems flee —

4

I would not paint – a picture –
I'd rather be the One
Its bright impossibility
To dwell – delicious – on –
And wonder how the fingers feel
Whose rare – celestial – stir –
Evokes so sweet a Torment –
Such sumptuous – Despair –

I would not talk, like Cornets –
I'd rather be the One
Raised softly to the Ceilings –
And out, and easy on –
Through Villages of Ether –
Myself endued Balloon
By but a lip of Metal –
The pier to my Pontoon –

Nor would I be a Poet –
It's finer – own the Ear –
Enamored – impotent – content –
The License to revere,
A privilege so awful
What would the Dower be,
Had I the Art to stun myself
With Bolts of Melody!

5

This was a Poet – It is That
Distills amazing sense
From ordinary Meanings –
And Attar so immense

From the familiar species
That perished by the Door –
We wonder it was not Ourselves
Arrested it – before –

Of Pictures, the Discloser –
The Poet – it is He –
Entitles Us – by Contrast –
To ceaseless Poverty –

Of Portion – so unconscious –
The Robbing – could not harm –
Himself – to Him – a Fortune –
Exterior – to Time –

6

She dealt her pretty words like Blades –
How glittering they shone –
And every One unbared a Nerve
Or wantoned with a Bone –

She never deemed – she hurt –
That – is not Steel's Affair –
A vulgar grimace in the Flesh –
How ill the Creatures bear –

To Ache is human – not polite –
The Film upon the eye
Mortality's old Custom –
Just locking up – to Die.

To pile like Thunder to its close
Then crumble grand away
While Everything created hid
This – would be Poetry –

Or Love – the two coeval come –
We both and neither prove –
Experience either and consume -
For None see God and live –

The Martyr Poets – did not tell –
But wrought their Pang in syllable –
That when their mortal name be numb –
Their mortal fate – encourage Some –

The Martyr Painters – never spoke –
Bequeathing – rather – to their Work –
That when their conscious fingers cease –
Some seek in Art – the Art of Peace –

I reckon – when I count at all –
First – Poets – Then the Sun –
Then Summer – Then the Heaven of God –
And then – the List is done –

But, looking back – the First so seems
To Comprehend the Whole –
The Others look a needless Show –
So I write – Poets – All –

Their Summer – lasts a Solid Year –
They can afford a Sun
The East – would deem extravagant –
And if the Further Heaven –

Be Beautiful as they prepare
For Those who worship Them –
It is too difficult a Grace –
To justify the Dream –

10

The Poets light but Lamps –
Themselves – go out –
The Wicks they stimulate –
If vital Light

Inhere as do the Suns –
Each Age a Lens
Disseminating their
Circumference –

The butterfly obtains
But little sympathy
Though favorably mentioned
In Entomology –

Because he travels freely
And wears a proper coat
The circumspect are certain
That he is dissolute –

Had he the homely scutcheon
Of modest Industry
'Twere fitter certifying
For Immortality –

We – Bee and I – live by the quaffing –
'Tisn't *all Hock* – with us –
Life has its *Ale* –
But it's many a lay of the Dim Burgundy –
We chant – for cheer – when the Wines – fail –

Do we "get drunk"?
Ask the jolly Clovers!
Do we "beat" our "Wife"?
I – never wed –
Bee – pledges *his* – in minute flagons –
Dainty – as the tress – on her deft Head –

While runs the Rhine –
He and I – revel –
First – at the vat – and latest at the Vine –
Noon – our last Cup –
"Found dead" – "of Nectar" –
By a humming Coroner –
In a By-Thyme!

13

A word is dead
When it is said,
Some say.

I say it just
Begins to live
That day.

14

A Word dropped careless on a Page
May stimulate an eye
When folded in perpetual seam
The Wrinkled Maker lie

Infection in the sentence breeds
We may inhale Despair
At distances of Centuries
From the Malaria –

Could mortal lip divine
The undeveloped Freight
Of a delivered syllable
'Twould crumble with the weight.

Speech is one symptom of Affection
And Silence one –
The perfectest communication
Is heard of none –

Exists and its indorsement
Is had within –
Behold, said the Apostle,
Yet had not seen!

To tell the Beauty would decrease
To state the Spell demean –
There is a syllable-less Sea
Of which it is the sign –
My will endeavors for its word
And fails, but entertains
A Rapture as of Legacies –
Of introspective Mines –

18

Those fair – fictitious People –
The Women – plucked away
From our familiar Lifetime –
The Men of Ivory –

Those Boys and Girls, in Canvas –
Who stay upon the Wall
In Everlasting Keepsake –
Can Anybody tell?

We trust – in places perfecter –
Inheriting Delight
Beyond our faint Conjecture –
Our dizzy Estimate –

Remembering ourselves, we trust –
Yet Blesseder – than We –
Through Knowing – where We only hope –
Receiving – where we – pray –

Of Expectation – also –
Anticipating us
With transport, that would be a pain
Except for Holiness –

Esteeming us – as Exile –
Themself – admitted Home –
Through easy Miracle of Death –
The Way ourself, must come –

19

Surgeons must be very careful
When they take the knife!
Underneath their fine incisions
Stirs the Culprit – *Life*!

Make me a picture of the sun –
So I can hang it in my room –
And make believe I'm getting warm
When others call it "Day"!

Draw me a Robin – on a stem –
So I am hearing him, I'll dream,
And when the Orchards stop their tune –
Put my pretense – away –

Say if it's really – warm at noon –
Whether it's Buttercups – that "skim" –
Or Butterflies – that "bloom"?
Then – skip – the frost – upon the lea –
And skip the Russet – on the tree –
Let's play those – never come!

21

Delight – becomes pictorial –
When viewed through Pain –
More fair – because impossible
That any gain –

The Mountain – at a given distance –
In Amber – lies –
Approached – the Amber flits – a little –
And That's – the Skies –

Your thoughts don't have words every day
They come a single time
Like signal esoteric sips
Of the communion Wine
Which while you taste so native seems
So easy so to be
You cannot comprehend its price
Nor its infrequency

I dwell in Possibility –
A fairer House than Prose –
More numerous of Windows –
Superior – for Doors –

Of Chambers as the Cedars –
Impregnable of Eye –
And for an Everlasting Roof
The Gambrels of the Sky –

Of Visitors – the fairest –
For Occupation – This –
The spreading wide my narrow Hands
To gather Paradise –

Me from Myself – to banish –
Had I Art –
Impregnable my Fortress
Unto All Heart –

But since Myself – assault Me –
How have I peace
Except by subjugating
Consciousness?

And since We're mutual Monarch
How this be
Except by Abdication –
Me – of Me?

It troubled me as once I was –
For I was once a Child –
Concluding how an Atom – fell –
And yet the Heavens – held –

The Heavens weighed the most – by far –
Yet Blue – and solid – stood –
Without a Bolt – that I could prove –
Would Giants – understand?

Life set me larger – problems –
Some I shall keep – to solve
Till Algebra is easier –
Or simpler proved – above –

Then – too – be comprehended –
What sorer – puzzled me –
Why Heaven did not break away –
And tumble – Blue – on me –

He found my Being – set it up –
Adjusted it to place –
Then carved his name – upon it –
And bade it to the East

Be faithful – in his absence –
And he would come again –
With Equipage of Amber –
That time – to take it Home –

I started Early – Took my Dog –
And visited the Sea –
The Mermaids in the Basement
Came out to look at me –

And Frigates – in the Upper Floor
Extended Hempen Hands –
Presuming Me to be a Mouse –
Aground – upon the Sands –

But no Man moved Me – till the Tide
Went past my simple Shoe –
And past my Apron – and my Belt
And past my Bodice – too –

And made as He would eat me up –
As wholly as a Dew
Upon a Dandelion's Sleeve –
And then – I started – too –

And He – He followed – close behind –
I felt His Silver Heel
Upon my Ankle – Then my Shoes
Would overflow with Pearl –

Until We met the Solid Town –
No One he seemed to know –
And bowing – with a Mighty look –
At me – The Sea withdrew –

Unto my Books – so good to turn –
Far ends of tired Days –
It half endears the Abstinence –
And Pain – is missed – in Praise –

As Flavors – cheer Retarded Guests
With Banquettings to be –
So Spices – stimulate the time
Till my small Library –

It may be Wilderness – without –
Far feet of failing Men –
But Holiday – excludes the night –
And it is Bells – within –

I thank these Kinsmen of the Shelf –
Their Countenances Kid
Enamor – in Prospective –
And satisfy – obtained –

Afraid! Of whom am I afraid?
Not Death – for who is He?
The Porter of my Father's Lodge
As much abasheth me!

Of Life? 'Twere odd I fear [a] thing
That comprehendeth me
In one or two existences –
As Deity decree –

Of Resurrection? Is the East
Afraid to trust the Morn
With her fastidious forehead?
As soon impeach my Crown!

It would have starved a Gnat –
To live so small as I –
And yet I was a living Child –
With Food's necessity

Upon me – like a Claw –
I could no more remove
Than I could coax a Leech away –
Or make a Dragon – move –

Nor like the Gnat – had I –
The privilege to fly
And seek a Dinner for myself –
How mightier He – than I –

Nor like Himself – the Art
Upon the Window Pane
To gad my little Being out –
And not begin – again –

They shut me up in Prose –
As when a little Girl
They put me in the Closet –
Because they liked me "still" –

Still! Could themself have peeped –
And seen my Brain – go round –
They might as wise have lodged a Bird
For Treason – in the Pound –

Himself has but to will
And easy as a Star
Abolish his Captivity –
And laugh – No more have I –

Don't put up my Thread and Needle –
I'll begin to Sew
When the Birds begin to whistle –
Better Stitches – so –

These were bent – my sight got crooked –
When my mind – is plain
I'll do seams – a Queen's endeavor
Would not blush to own –

Hems – too fine for Lady's tracing
To the sightless Knot –
Tucks – of dainty interspersion –
Like a dotted Dot –

Leave my Needle in the furrow –
Where I put it down –
I can make the zigzag stitches
Straight – when I am strong –

Till then – dreaming I am sewing
Fetch the seam I missed –
Closer – so I – at my sleeping –
Still surmise I stitch –

They called me to the Window, for
"'Twas Sunset" – Some one said –
I only saw a Sapphire Farm –
And just a Single Herd –

Of Opal Cattle – feeding far
Upon so vain a Hill –
As even while I looked – dissolved –
Nor Cattle were – nor Soil –

But in their stead – a Sea – displayed –
And Ships – of such a size
As Crew of Mountains – could afford –
And Decks – to seat the skies –

This – too – the Showman rubbed away –
And when I looked again –
Nor Farm – nor Opal Herd – was there –
Nor Mediterranean –

I cannot live with You –
It would be Life –
And Life is over there –
Behind the Shelf

The Sexton keeps the Key to –
Putting up
Our Life – His Porcelain –
Like a Cup –

Discarded of the Housewife –
Quaint – or Broke –
A newer Sevres pleases –
Old Ones crack –

I could not die – with You –
For One must wait
To shut the Other's Gaze down –
You – could not –

And I – Could I stand by
And see You – freeze –
Without my Right of Frost –
Death's privilege?

Nor could I rise – with You –
Because Your Face
Would put out Jesus' –
That New Grace

Glow plain – and foreign
On my homesick Eye –
Except that You than He
Shone closer by –

They'd judge Us – How –
For You – served Heaven – You know,
Or sought to –
I could not –

Because You saturated Sight –
And I had no more Eyes
For sordid excellence
As Paradise

And were You lost, I would be –
Though My Name
Rang loudest
On the Heavenly fame –

And were You – saved –
And I – condemned to be
Where You were not –
That self – were Hell to Me –

So We must meet apart –
You there – I – here –
With just the Door ajar
That Oceans are – and Prayer –
And that White Sustenance –
Despair –

She dwelleth in the Ground –
Where Daffodils – abide –
Her Maker – Her Metropolis –
The Universe – Her Maid –

To fetch Her Grace – and Hue –
And Fairness – and Renown –
The Firmament's – To Pluck Her –
And fetch Her Thee – be mine –

To be alive – is Power –
Existence – in itself –
Without a further function –
Omnipotence – Enough –

To be alive – and Will!
'Tis able as a God –
The Maker – of Ourselves – be what –
Such being Finitude!

Each Life Converges to some Centre –
Expressed – or still –
Exists in every Human Nature
A Goal –

Embodied scarcely to itself – it may be –
Too fair
For Credibility's presumption
To mar –

Adored with caution – as a Brittle Heaven –
To reach
Were hopeless, as the Rainbow's Raiment
To touch –

Yet persevered toward – sure – for the Distance –
How high –
Unto the Saints' slow diligence –
The Sky –

Ungained – it may be – by a Life's low Venture –
But then –
Eternity enable the endeavoring
Again.

I tie my Hat – I crease my Shawl –
Life's little duties do – precisely –
As the very least
Were infinite – to me –

I put new Blossoms in the Glass –
And throw the old – away –
I push a petal from my Gown
That anchored there – I weigh
The time 'twill be till six o'clock
I have so much to do –
And yet – Existence – some way back –
Stopped – struck – my ticking – through –
We cannot put Ourself away
As a completed Man
Or Woman – When the Errand's done
We came to Flesh – upon –
There may be – Miles on Miles of Nought –
Of Action – sicker far –
To simulate – is stinging work –
To cover what we are
From Science – and from Surgery –
Too Telescopic Eyes
To bear on us unshaded –

For their – sake – not for Ours –
'Twould start them –
We – could tremble –
But since we got a Bomb –
And held it in our Bosom –
Nay – Hold it – it is calm –

Therefore – we do life's labor –
Though life's Reward – be done –
With scrupulous exactness –
To hold our Senses – on –

Pain – has an Element of Blank –
It cannot recollect
When it begun – or if there were
A time when it was not –

It has no Future – but itself –
Its Infinite contain
Its Past – enlightened to perceive
New Periods – of Pain.

40

A nearness to Tremendousness –
An Agony procures –
Affliction ranges Boundlessness –
Vicinity to Laws

Contentment's quiet Suburb –
Affliction cannot stay
In Acres – Its Location
Is Illocality –

'Twas such a little – little boat
That toddled down the bay!
'Twas such a gallant – gallant sea
That beckoned it away!

'Twas such a greedy, greedy wave
That licked it from the Coast –
Nor ever guessed the stately sails
My little craft was *lost*!

The nearest Dream recedes – unrealized –
The Heaven we chase,
Like the June Bee – before the School Boy,
Invites the Race –
Stoops – to an easy Clover –
Dips – evades – teases – deploys –
Then – to the Royal Clouds
Lifts his light Pinnace –
Heedless of the Boy –
Staring – bewildered – at the mocking sky –
Homesick for steadfast Honey –
Ah, the Bee flies not
That brews that rare variety!

All the letters I can write
Are not fair as this –
Syllables of Velvet –
Sentences of Plush,
Depths of Ruby, undrained,
Hid, Lip, for Thee –
Play it were a Humming Bird –
And just sipped – me –

Struck, was I, not yet by Lightning –
Lightning – lets away
Power to perceive His Process
With Vitality.

Maimed – was I – yet not by Venture –
Stone of stolid Boy –
Nor a Sportsman's Peradventure –
Who mine Enemy?

Robbed – was I – intact to Bandit –
All my Mansion torn –
Sun – withdrawn to Recognition –
Furthest shining – done –

Yet was not the foe – of any –
Not the smallest Bird
In the nearest Orchard dwelling
Be of Me – afraid.

Most – I love the Cause that slew Me.
Often as I die
Its beloved Recognition
Holds a Sun on Me –

Best – at Setting – as is Nature's –
Neither witnessed Rise
Till the infinite Aurora
In the other's eyes.

Again – his voice is at the door –
I feel the old *Degree* –
I hear him ask the servant
For such an one – as me –

I take a *flower* – as I go –
My face to *justify* –
He never *saw* me – *in this life* –
I might *surprise* his eye!

I cross the Hall with *mingled* steps –
I – silent – pass the door –
I look on all this world *contains* –
Just his face – nothing more!

We talk in *careless* – and in *toss* –
A kind of *plummet* strain –
Each – sounding – shyly –
Just – how – deep –
The *other's* one – had been –

We *walk* – I leave my Dog – at home –
A *tender* – *thoughtful* Moon
Goes with us – just a little way –
And – then – we are *alone* –

Alone – if *Angels* are "alone" –
First time they *try* the *sky*!
Alone – if those "veiled faces" – be –
We cannot *count* – on High!

I'd give – to live that hour – *again* –
The *purple* – *in my Vein* –
But *He* must *count the drops* – *himself* –
My price for *every stain*!

THE WORKS OF
LOVE

46

Who occupies this House?
A Stranger I must judge
Since No one knows His Circumstance –
'Tis well the name and age

Are writ upon the Door
Or I should fear to pause
Where not so much as Honest Dog
Approach encourages.

It seems a curious Town –
Some Houses very old,
Some – newly raised this Afternoon,
Were I compelled to build

It should not be among
Inhabitants so still
But where the Birds assemble
And Boys were possible.

Before Myself was born
'Twas settled, so they say,
A Territory for the Ghosts –
And Squirrels, formerly.

Until a Pioneer, as
Settlers often do
Liking the quiet of the Place
Attracted more unto –

And from a Settlement
A Capital has grown
Distinguished for the gravity
Of every Citizen.

The Owner of this House
A Stranger He must be –
Eternity's Acquaintances
Are mostly so – to me.

Drab Habitation of Whom?
Tabernacle or Tomb –
Or Dome of Worm –
Or Porch of Gnome –
Or some Elf's Catacomb?

There is a solitude of space
A solitude of sea
A solitude of death, but these
Society shall be
Compared with that profounder site
That polar privacy
A soul admitted to itself –
Finite infinity.

A little Snow was here and there
Disseminated in her Hair –
Since she and I had met and played
Decade had gathered to Decade –

But Time had added not obtained
Impregnable the Rose
For summer too indelible
Too obdurate for Snows –

Abraham to kill him
Was distinctly told –
Isaac was an Urchin –
Abraham was old –

Not a hesitation –
Abraham complied –
Flattered by Obeisance
Tyranny demurred –

Isaac – to his children
Lived to tell the tale –
Moral – with a Mastiff
Manners may prevail.

51

What we see we know somewhat
Be it but a little –
What we don't surmise we do
Though it shows so fickle

I shall vote for Lands with Locks
Granted I can pick 'em –
Transport's doubtful Dividend
Patented by Adam.

The Drop, that wrestles in the Sea –
Forgets her own locality –
As I – toward Thee –

She knows herself an incense small –
Yet *small* – she sighs – if *All* – is *All* –
How *larger* – be?

The Ocean – smiles – at her Conceit –
But *she*, forgetting Amphitrite –
Pleads – "Me"?

53

All overgrown by cunning moss,
All interspersed with weed,
The little cage of "Currer Bell"
In quiet "Haworth" laid.

Gathered from many wanderings –
Gethsemane can tell
Thro' what transporting anguish
She reached the Asphodel!

Soft fall the sounds of Eden
Upon her puzzled ear –
Oh what an afternoon for Heaven,
When "Bronte" entered there!

54

I should not dare to leave my friend,
Because – because if he should die
While I was gone – and I – too late –
Should reach the Heart that wanted me –

If I should disappoint the eyes
That hunted – hunted so – to see –
And could not bear to shut until
They "noticed" me – they noticed me –

If I should stab the patient faith
So sure I'd come – so sure I'd come –
It *listening* – listening – went to sleep –
Telling my tardy name –

My Heart would wish it broke before –
Since breaking then – since breaking then –
Were useless as next morning's sun –
Where midnight frosts – had lain!

A little East of Jordan,
Evangelists record,
A Gymnast and an Angel
Did wrestle long and hard –

Till morning touching mountain –
And Jacob, waxing strong,
The Angel begged permission
To Breakfast – to return –

Not so, said cunning Jacob!
"I will not let thee go
Except thou bless me" – Stranger!
The which acceded to –

Light swung the silver fleeces
"Peniel" Hills beyond,
And the bewildered Gymnast
Found he had worsted God!

When I was small, a Woman died –
Today – her Only Boy
Went up from the Potomac –
His face all Victory

To look at her – How slowly
The Seasons must have turned
Till Bullets clipt an Angle
And He passed quickly round –

If pride shall be in Paradise –
Ourself cannot decide –
Of their imperial Conduct –
No person testified –

But, proud in Apparition –
That Woman and her Boy
Pass back and forth, before my Brain
As even in the sky –

I'm confident that Bravoes –
Perpetual break abroad
For Braveries, remote as this
In Scarlet Maryland –

57

A long – long Sleep – A famous – Sleep –
That makes no show for Morn –
By Stretch of Limb – or stir of Lid –
An independent One –

Was ever idleness like This?
Upon a Bank of Stone
To bask the Centuries away –
Nor once look up – for Noon?

We talked as Girls do –
Fond, and late –
We speculated fair, on every subject, but the
Grave –
Of ours, none affair –

We handled Destinies, as cool –
As we – Disposers – be –
And God, a Quiet Party
To our Authority –

But fondest, dwelt upon Ourself
As we eventual – be –
When Girls to Women, softly raised
We – occupy – Degree –

We parted with a contract
To cherish, and to write
But Heaven made both, impossible
Before another night.

59

The Sweets of Pillage, can be known
To no one but the Thief –
Compassion for Integrity
Is his divinest Grief –

60

A Prison gets to be a friend –
Between its Ponderous face
And Ours – a Kinsmanship express –
And in its narrow Eyes –

We come to look with gratitude
For the appointed Beam
It deal us – stated as our food –
And hungered for – the same –

We learn to know the Planks –
That answer to Our feet –
So miserable a sound – at first –
Nor ever now – so sweet –

As plashing in the Pools –
When Memory was a Boy –
But a Demurer Circuit –
A Geometric Joy –

The Posture of the Key
That interrupt the Day
To Our Endeavor – Not so real
The Cheek of Liberty –

As this Phantasm Steel –
Whose features – Day and Night –
Are present to us – as Our Own –
And as escapeless – quite –

The narrow Round – the Stint –
The slow exchange of Hope –
For something passiver – Content
Too steep for looking up –

The Liberty we knew
Avoided – like a Dream –
Too wide for any Night but Heaven –
If That – indeed – redeem –

Her final Summer was it –
And yet We guessed it not –
If tenderer industriousness
Pervaded Her, We thought

A further force of life
Developed from within –
When Death lit all the shortness up
It made the hurry plain –

We wondered at our blindness
When nothing was to see
But Her Carrara Guide post –
At Our Stupidity –

When duller than our dullness
The Busy Darling lay –
So busy was she – finishing –
So leisurely – were We –

I Years had been from Home
And now before the Door
I dared not enter, lest a Face
I never saw before

Stare stolid into mine
And ask my Business there –
"My Business but a Life I left
Was such remaining there?"

I leaned upon the Awe –
I lingered with Before –
The Second like an Ocean rolled
And broke against my ear –

I laughed a crumbling Laugh
That I could fear a Door
Who Consternation compassed
And never winced before.

I fitted to the Latch
My Hand, with trembling care
Lest back the awful Door should spring
And leave me in the Floor –

Then moved my Fingers off
As cautiously as Glass
And held my ears, and like a Thief
Fled gasping from the House –

Papa above!
Regard a Mouse
O'erpowered by the Cat!
Reserve within thy kingdom
A "Mansion" for the Rat!

Snug in seraphic Cupboards
To nibble all the day,
While unsuspecting Cycles
Wheel solemnly away!

She sights a Bird – she chuckles –
She flattens – then she crawls –
She runs without the look of feet –
Her eyes increase to Balls –

Her Jaws stir – twitching – hungry –
Her Teeth can hardly stand –
She leaps, but Robin leaped the first –
Ah, Pussy, of the Sand,

The Hopes so juicy ripening –
You almost bathed your Tongue –
When Bliss disclosed a hundred Toes –
And fled with every one –

A little Dog that wags his tail
And knows no other joy
Of such a little Dog am I
Reminded by a Boy

Who gambols all the living Day
Without an earthly cause
Because he is a little Boy
I honestly suppose –

The Cat that in the Corner dwells
Her martial Day forgot
The Mouse but a Tradition now
Of her desireless Lot

Another class remind me
Who neither please nor play
But not to make a "bit of noise"
Beseech each little Boy –

Civilization – spurns – the Leopard!
Was the Leopard – bold?
Deserts – never rebuked her Satin –
Ethiop – her Gold –
Tawny – her Customs –
She was Conscious –
Spotted – her Dun Gown –
This was the Leopard's nature – Signor –
Need – a keeper – frown?

Pity – the Pard – that left her Asia –
Memories – of Palm –
Cannot be stifled – with Narcotic –
Nor suppressed – with Balm –

Within my Garden, rides a Bird
Upon a single Wheel –
Whose spokes a dizzy Music make
As 'twere a travelling Mill –

He never stops, but slackens
Above the Ripest Rose –
Partakes without alighting
And praises as he goes,

Till every spice is tasted –
And then his Fairy Gig
Reels in remoter atmospheres –
And I rejoin my Dog,

And He and I, perplex us
If positive, 'twere we –
Or bore the Garden in the Brain
This Curiosity –

But He, the best Logician,
Refers my clumsy eye –
To just vibrating Blossoms!
An Exquisite Reply!

A Rat surrendered here
A brief career of Cheer
And Fraud and Fear.

Of Ignominy's due
Let all addicted to
Beware.

The most obliging Trap
Its tendency to snap
Cannot resist –

Temptation is the Friend
Repugnantly resigned
At last.

The Rat is the concisest Tenant.
He pays no Rent.
Repudiates the Obligation –
On Schemes intent

Balking our Wit
To sound or circumvent –
Hate cannot harm
A Foe so reticent –
Neither Decree prohibit him –
Lawful as Equilibrium.

As the Starved Maelstrom laps the Navies
As the Vulture teased
Forces the Broods in lonely Valleys
As the Tiger eased

By but a Crumb of Blood, fasts Scarlet
Till he meet a Man
Dainty adorned with Veins and Tissues
And partakes – his Tongue

Cooled by the Morsel for a moment
Grows a fiercer thing
Till he esteem his Dates and Cocoa
A Nutrition mean

I, of a finer Famine
Deem my Supper dry
For but a Berry of Domingo
And a Torrid Eye.

The Judge is like the Owl –
I've heard my Father tell –
And Owls do build in Oaks –
So here's an Amber Sill –

That slanted in my Path –
When going to the Barn –
And if it serve You for a House –
Itself is not in vain –

About the price – 'tis small –
I only ask a Tune
At Midnight – Let the Owl select
His favorite Refrain.

One of the ones that Midas touched
Who failed to touch us all
Was that confiding Prodigal
The reeling Oriole –

So drunk he disavows it
With badinage divine –
So dazzling we mistake him
For an alighting Mine –

A Pleader – a Dissembler –
An Epicure – a Thief –
Betimes an Oratorio –
An Ecstasy in chief –

The Jesuit of Orchards
He cheats as he enchants
Of an entire Attar
For his decamping wants –

The splendor of a Burmah
The Meteor of Birds,
Departing like a Pageant
Of Ballads and of Bards –

I never thought that Jason sought
For any Golden Fleece
But then I am a rural man
With thoughts that make for Peace –

But if there were a Jason,
Tradition bear with me
Behold his lost Aggrandizement
Upon the Apple Tree –

A Bird came down the Walk –
He did not know I saw –
He bit an Angleworm in halves
And ate the fellow, raw,

And then he drank a Dew
From a convenient Grass –
And then hopped sidewise to the Wall
To let a Beetle pass –

He glanced with rapid eyes
That hurried all around –
They looked like frightened Beads, I thought –
He stirred his Velvet Head

Like one in danger, Cautious,
I offered him a Crumb
And he unrolled his feathers
And rowed him softer home –

Than Oars divide the Ocean,
Too silver for a seam –
Or Butterflies, off Banks of Noon
Leap, plashless as they swim.

74

The Robin for the Crumb
Returns no syllable
But long records the Lady's name
In Silver Chronicle.

Upon his Saddle sprung a Bird
And crossed a thousand Trees
Before a Fence without a Fare
His Fantasy did please
And then he lifted up his Throat
And squandered such a Note
A Universe that overheard
Is stricken by it yet —

To hear an Oriole sing
May be a common thing –
Or only a divine.

It is not of the Bird
Who sings the same, unheard,
As unto Crowd –

The Fashion of the Ear
Attireth that it hear
In Dun, or fair –

So whether it be Rune,
Or whether it be none
Is of within.

The "Tune is in the Tree –"
The Skeptic – showeth me –
"No Sir! In Thee!"

The Birds begun at Four o'clock –
Their period for Dawn –
A Music numerous as space –
But neighboring as Noon –

I could not count their Force –
Their Voices did expend
As Brook by Brook bestows itself
To multiply the Pond.

Their Witnesses were not –
Except occasional man –
In homely industry arrayed –
To overtake the Morn –

Nor was it for applause –
That I could ascertain –
But independent Ecstasy
Of Deity and Men –

By Six, the Flood had done –
No Tumult there had been
Of Dressing, or Departure –
And yet the Band was gone –

The Sun engrossed the East –
The Day controlled the World –
The Miracle that introduced
Forgotten, as fulfilled.

At Half past Three, a single Bird
Unto a silent Sky
Propounded but a single term
Of cautious melody.

At Half past Four, Experiment
Had subjugated test
And lo, Her silver Principle
Supplanted all the rest.

At Half past Seven, Element
Nor Implement, be seen –
And Place was where the Presence was
Circumference between.

She staked her Feathers – Gained an Arc –
Debated – Rose again –
This time – beyond the estimate
Of Envy, or of Men –

And now, among Circumference –
Her steady Boat be seen –
At home – among the Billows – As
The Bough where she was born –

One Joy of so much anguish
Sweet nature has for me
I shun it as I do Despair
Or dear iniquity –
Why Birds, a Summer morning
Before the Quick of Day
Should stab my ravished spirit
With Dirks of Melody
Is part of an inquiry
That will receive reply
When Flesh and Spirit sunder
In Death's Immediately –

The Bird her punctual music brings
And lays it in its place –
Its place is in the Human Heart
And in the Heavenly Grace –
What respite from her thrilling toil
Did Beauty ever take –
But Work might be electric Rest
To those that Magic make –

Most she touched me by her muteness –
Most she won me by the way
She presented her small figure –
Plea itself – for Charity –

Were a Crumb my whole possession –
Were there famine in the land –
Were it my resource from starving –
Could I such a plea withstand –

Not upon her knee to thank me
Sank this Beggar from the Sky –
But the Crumb partook – departed –
And returned On High –

I supposed – when sudden
Such a Praise began
'Twas as Space sat singing
To herself – and men –

'Twas the Winged Beggar –
Afterward I learned
To her Benefactor
Making Gratitude

A prompt – executive Bird is the Jay –
Bold as a Bailiff's Hymn –
Brittle and Brief in quality –
Warrant in every line –

Sitting a Bough like a Brigadier
Confident and straight –
Much is the mien of him in March
As a Magistrate –

No Brigadier throughout the Year
So civic as the Jay –
A Neighbor and a Warrior too
With shrill felicity
Pursuing Winds that censure us
A February Day,
The Brother of the Universe
Was never blown away –
The Snow and he are intimate –
I've often seen them play
When Heaven looked upon us all
With such severity
I felt apology were due
To an insulted sky
Whose pompous frown was Nutriment
To their Temerity –
The Pillow of this daring Head
Is pungent Evergreens –
His Larder – terse and Militant –
Unknown – refreshing things –
His Character – a Tonic –
His future – a Dispute –
Unfair an Immortality
That leaves this Neighbor out –

An Antiquated Tree
Is cherished of the Crow
Because that Junior Foliage is disrespectful now
To venerable Birds
Whose Corporation Coat
Would decorate Oblivion's
Remotest Consulate.

Bee! I'm expecting you!
Was saying Yesterday
To Somebody you know
That you were due –

The Frogs got Home last Week –
Are settled, and at work –
Birds, mostly back –
The Clover warm and thick –

You'll get my Letter by
The seventeenth; Reply
Or better, be with me –
Yours, Fly.

The Butterfly in honored Dust
Assuredly will lie
But none will pass the Catacomb
So chastened as the Fly –

The Bat is dun, with wrinkled Wings –
Like fallow Article –
And not a song pervade his Lips –
Or none perceptible.

His small Umbrella quaintly halved
Describing in the Air
An Arc alike inscrutable
Elate Philosopher.

Deputed from what Firmament –
Of what Astute Abode –
Empowered with what Malignity
Auspiciously withheld –

To his adroit Creator
Ascribe no less the praise –
Beneficent, believe me,
His Eccentricities –

How soft a Caterpillar steps –
I find one on my Hand
From such a velvet world it comes
Such plushes at command
Its soundless travels just arrest
My slow – terrestrial eye
Intent upon its own career
What use has it for me –

A winged spark doth soar about –
I never met it near
For Lightning it is oft mistook
When nights are hot and sere –

Its twinkling Travels it pursues
Above the Haunts of men –
A speck of Rapture – first perceived
By feeling it is gone –
Rekindled by some action quaint

The Spider holds a Silver Ball
In unperceived Hands –
And dancing softly to Himself
His Yarn of Pearl – unwinds –

He plies from Nought to Nought –
In unsubstantial Trade –
Supplants our Tapestries with His –
In half the period –

An Hour to rear supreme
His Continents of Light –
Then dangle from the Housewife's Broom –
His Boundaries – forgot –

A Spider sewed at Night
Without a Light
Upon an Arc of White.

If Ruff it was of Dame
Or Shroud of Gnome
Himself himself inform.

Of Immortality
His Strategy
Was Physiognomy.

The Spider as an Artist
Has never been employed –
Though his surpassing Merit
Is freely certified

By every Broom and Bridget
Throughout a Christian Land –
Neglected Son of Genius
I take thee by the Hand –

His Mansion in the Pool
The Frog forsakes –
He rises on a Log
And statements makes –
His Auditors two Worlds
Deducting me –
The Orator of April
Is hoarse Today –
His Mittens at his Feet
No Hand hath he –
His eloquence a Bubble
As Fame should be –
Applaud him to discover
To your chagrin
Demosthenes has vanished
In Waters Green –

95

I'm Nobody! Who are you?
Are you – Nobody – Too?
Then there's a pair of us?
Don't tell! they'd advertise – you know!

How dreary – to be – Somebody!
How public – like a Frog –
To tell one's name – the livelong June –
To an admiring Bog!

The long sigh of the Frog
Upon a Summer's Day
Enacts intoxication
Upon the Revery –
But his receding Swell
Substantiates a Peace
That makes the Ear inordinate
For corporal release –

His Feet are shod with Gauze –
His Helmet, is of Gold,
His Breast, a Single Onyx
With Chrysophrase, inlaid.

His Labor is a Chant –
His Idleness – a Tune –
Oh, for a Bee's experience
Of Clovers, and of Noon!

98

Like Trains of Cars on Tracks of Plush
I hear the level Bee –
A Jar across the Flowers goes
Their Velvet Masonry

Withstands until the sweet Assault
Their Chivalry consumes –
While He, victorious tilts away
To vanquish other Blooms.

Bees are Black, with Gilt Surcingles –
Buccaneers of Buzz.
Ride abroad in ostentation
And subsist on Fuzz.

Fuzz ordained – not Fuzz contingent –
Marrows of the Hill.
Jugs – a Universe's fracture
Could not jar or spill.

His little Hearse like Figure
Unto itself a Dirge
To a delusive Lilac
The vanity divulge
Of Industry and Morals
And every righteous thing
For the divine Perdition
Of Idleness and Spring –

A feather from the Whippoorwill
That everlasting – sings!
Whose galleries – are Sunrise –
Whose Opera – the Springs –
Whose Emerald Nest the Ages spin
Of mellow – murmuring thread –
Whose Beryl Egg, what Schoolboys hunt
In "Recess" – Overhead!

102

These are the Nights that Beetles love —
From Eminence remote
Drives ponderous perpendicular
His figure intimate
The terror of the Children
The merriment of men
Depositing his Thunder
He hoists abroad again —
A Bomb upon the Ceiling
Is an improving thing —
It keeps the nerves progressive
Conjecture flourishing —
Too dear the Summer evening
Without discreet alarm —
Supplied by Entomology
With its remaining charm —

Bring me the sunset in a cup,
Reckon the morning's flagons up
And say how many Dew,
Tell me how far the morning leaps –
Tell me what time the weaver sleeps
Who spun the breadths of blue!

Write me how many notes there be
In the new Robin's ecstasy
Among astonished boughs –
How many trips the Tortoise makes –
How many cups the Bee partakes,
The Debauchee of Dews!

Also, who laid the Rainbow's piers,
Also, who leads the docile spheres
By withes of supple blue?
Whose fingers string the stalactite –
Who counts the wampum of the night
To see that none is due?

Who built this little Alban House
And shut the windows down so close
My spirit cannot see?
Who'll let me out some gala day
With implements to fly away,
Passing Pomposity?

104

Conjecturing a Climate
Of unsuspended Suns –
Adds poignancy to Winter –
The Shivering Fancy turns

To a fictitious Country
To palliate a Cold –
Not obviated of Degree –
Nor eased – of Latitude –

105

From Cocoon forth a Butterfly
As Lady from her Door
Emerged – a Summer Afternoon –
Repairing Everywhere –

Without Design – that I could trace
Except to stray abroad
On Miscellaneous Enterprise
The Clovers – understood –

Her pretty Parasol be seen
Contracting in a Field
Where Men made Hay –
Then struggling hard
With an opposing Cloud –

Where Parties – Phantom as Herself –
To Nowhere – seemed to go
In purposeless Circumference –
As 'twere a Tropic Show –

And notwithstanding Bee – that worked –
And Flower – that zealous blew –
This Audience of Idleness
Disdained them, from the Sky –

Till Sundown crept – a steady Tide –
And Men that made the Hay –
And Afternoon – and Butterfly –
Extinguished – in the Sea –

"Nature" is what we see –
The Hill – the Afternoon –
Squirrel – Eclipse – the Bumble bee –
Nay – Nature is Heaven –
Nature is what we hear –
The Bobolink – the Sea –
Thunder – the Cricket –
Nay – Nature is Harmony –
Nature is what we know –
Yet have no art to say –
So impotent Our Wisdom is
To her Simplicity.

The Sun kept stooping – stooping – low!
The Hills to meet him rose!
On his side, what Transaction!
On their side, what Repose!

Deeper and deeper grew the stain
Upon the window pane –
Thicker and thicker stood the feet
Until the Tyrian

Was crowded dense with Armies –
So gay, so Brigadier –
That *I* felt martial stirrings
Who once the Cockade wore –
Charged, from my chimney corner –
But Nobody was there!

The Murmur of a Bee
A Witchcraft – yieldeth me –
If any ask me why –
'Twere easier to die –
Than tell –

The Red upon the Hill
Taketh away my will –
If anybody sneer –
Take care – for God is here –
That's all.

The Breaking of the Day
Addeth to my Degree –
If any ask me how –
Artist – who drew me so –
Must tell!

Some things that fly there be –
Birds – Hours – the Bumblebee –
Of these no Elegy.

Some things that stay there be –
Grief – Hills – Eternity –
Nor this behooveth me.

There are that resting, rise.
Can I expound the skies?
How still the Riddle lies!

If I should cease to bring a Rose
Upon a festal day,
'Twill be because *beyond* the Rose
I have been called away –

If I should cease to take the names
My buds commemorate –
'Twill be because *Death's* finger
Claps my murmuring lip!

111

A little Madness in the Spring
Is wholesome even for the King,
But God be with the Clown –
Who ponders this tremendous scene –
This whole Experiment of Green –
As if it were his own!

A Moth the hue of this
Haunts Candles in Brazil.
Nature's Experience would make
Our Reddest Second pale.

Nature is fond, I sometimes think,
Of Trinkets, as a Girl.

March is the Month of Expectation.
The things we do not know –
The Persons of prognostication
Are coming now –
We try to show becoming firmness –
But pompous Joy
Betrays us, as his first Betrothal
Betrays a Boy.

114

How lonesome the Wind must feel Nights –
When people have put out the Lights
And everything that has an Inn
Closes the shutter and goes in –

How pompous the Wind must feel Noons
Stepping to incorporeal Tunes
Correcting errors of the sky
And clarifying scenery

How mighty the Wind must feel Morns
Encamping on a thousand dawns
Espousing each and spurning all
Then soaring to his Temple Tall –

It was a quiet seeming Day –
There was no harm in earth or sky –
Till with the closing sun
There strayed an accidental Red
A Strolling Hue, one would have said
To westward of the Town --
But when the Earth began to jar
And Houses vanished with a roar
And Human Nature hid
We comprehended by the Awe
As those that Dissolution saw
The Poppy in the Cloud

Summer has two Beginnings –
Beginning once in June –
Beginning in October
Affectingly again –

Without, perhaps, the Riot
But graphicker for Grace –
As finer is a going
Than a remaining Face –

Departing then – forever –
Forever – until May –
Forever is deciduous –
Except to those who die –

The Gentian has a parched Corolla –
Like azure dried
'Tis Nature's buoyant juices
Beatified –
Without a vaunt or sheen
As casual as Rain
And as benign –

When most is past – it comes –
Nor isolate it seems
Its Bond its Friend –
To fill its Fringed career
And aid an aged Year
Abundant end –

Its lot – were it forgot –
This Truth endear –
Fidelity is gain
Creation o'er –

118

A chilly Peace infests the Grass
The Sun respectful lies –
Not any Trance of industry
These shadows scrutinize –

Whose Allies go no more astray
For service or for Glee –
But all mankind deliver here
From whatsoever sea –

Summer begins to have the look
Peruser of enchanting Book
Reluctantly but sure perceives
A gain upon the backward leaves —

Autumn begins to be inferred
By millinery of the cloud
Or deeper color in the shawl
That wraps the everlasting hill.

The eye begins its avarice
A meditation chastens speech
Some Dyer of a distant tree
Resumes his gaudy industry.

Conclusion is the course of All
At *most* to be perennial
And then elude stability
Recalls to immortality.

With sweetness unabated
Informed the hour had come
With no remiss of triumph
The autumn started home

Her home to be with Nature
As competition done
By influential kinsmen
Invited to return –

In supplements of Purple
An adequate repast
In heavenly reviewing
Her residue be past –

The farthest Thunder that I heard
Was nearer than the Sky
And rumbles still, though torrid Noons
Have lain their missiles by –
The Lightning that preceded it
Struck no one but myself –
But I would not exchange the Bolt
For all the rest of Life –
Indebtedness to Oxygen
The Happy may repay,
But not the obligation
To Electricity –
It founds the Homes and decks the Days
And every clamor bright
Is but the gleam concomitant
Of that waylaying Light –
The thought is quiet as a Flake –
A Crash without a Sound,
How Life's reverberation
Its Explanation found –

A Wind that rose
Though not a Leaf
In any Forest stirred
But with itself did cold engage
Beyond the Realm of Bird –
A Wind that woke a lone Delight
Like Separation's Swell
Restored in Arctic Confidence
To the Invisible –

Like Brooms of Steel
The Snow and Wind
Had swept the Winter Street –
The House was hooked
The Sun sent out
Faint Deputies of Heat –
Where rode the Bird
The Silence tied
His ample – plodding Steed
The Apple in the Cellar snug
Was all the one that played.

To interrupt His Yellow Plan
The Sun does not allow
Caprices of the Atmosphere –
And even when the Snow

Heaves Balls of Specks, like Vicious Boy
Directly in His Eye –
Does not so much as turn His Head
Busy with Majesty –

'Tis His to stimulate the Earth –
And magnetize the Sea –
And bind Astronomy, in place,
Yet Any passing by

Would deem Ourselves – the busier
As the Minutest Bee
That rides – emits a Thunder –
A Bomb – to justify –

It makes no difference abroad –
The Seasons – fit – the same –
The Mornings blossom into Noons –
And split their Pods of Flame –

Wild flowers – kindle in the Woods –
The Brooks slam – all the Day –
No Black bird bates his Banjo –
For passing Calvary –

Auto da Fe – and Judgment –
Are nothing to the Bee –
His separation from His Rose –
To Him – sums Misery –

So much Summer
Me for showing
Illegitimate –
Would a Smile's minute bestowing
Too exorbitant

To the Lady
With the Guinea
Look – if She should know
Crumb of Mine
A Robin's Larder
Would suffice to stow –

The Trees like Tassels – hit – and swung –
There seemed to rise a Tune
From Miniature Creatures
Accompanying the Sun –

Far Psalteries of Summer –
Enamoring the Ear
They never yet did satisfy –
Remotest – when most fair

The Sun shone whole at intervals –
Then Half – then utter hid –
As if Himself were optional
And had Estates of Cloud

Sufficient to enfold Him
Eternally from view –
Except it were a whim of His
To let the Orchards grow –

A Bird sat careless on the fence –
One gossipped in the Lane
On silver matters charmed a Snake
Just winding round a Stone –

Bright Flowers slit a Calyx
And soared upon a Stem
Like Hindered Flags – Sweet hoisted –
With Spices – in the Hem –

'Twas more – I cannot mention –
How mean – to those that see –
Vandyke's Delineation
Of Nature's – Summer Day!

These the days when Birds come back –
A very few – a Bird or two –
To take a backward look.

These are the days when skies resume
The old – old sophistries of June –
A blue and gold mistake.

Oh fraud that cannot cheat the Bee –
Almost thy plausibility
Induces my belief.

Till ranks of seeds their witness bear –
And softly thro' the altered air
Hurries a timid leaf.

Oh Sacrament of summer days,
Oh Last Communion in the Haze –
Permit a child to join.

Thy sacred emblems to partake –
Thy consecrated bread to take
And thine immortal wine!

Flowers – Well – if anybody
Can the ecstasy define –
Half a transport – half a trouble –
With which flowers humble men:
Anybody find the fountain
From which floods so contra flow –
I will give him all the Daisies
Which upon the hillside blow.

Too much pathos in their faces
For a simple breast like mine –
Butterflies from St. Domingo
Cruising round the purple line –
Have a system of aesthetics –
Far superior to mine.

A slash of Blue –
A sweep of Gray –
Some scarlet patches on the way,
Compose an Evening Sky –
A little purple – slipped between –
Some Ruby Trousers hurried on –
A Wave of Gold –
A Bank of Day –
This just makes out the Morning Sky.

131

A Burdock – clawed my Gown –
Not *Burdock's* – blame –
But *mine* –
Who went too near
The Burdock's *Den* –

A *Bog* – affronts my shoe –
What *else* have Bogs – *to do* –
The only Trade they *know* –
The *splashing Men*!
Ah, *pity* – *then*!

'Tis *Minnows can despise*!
The *Elephant's* – calm eyes
Look *further on*!

I dreaded that first Robin, so,
But He is mastered, now,
I'm some accustomed to Him grown,
He hurts a little, though –

I thought if I could only live
Till that first Shout got by –
Not all Pianos in the Woods
Had power to mangle me –

I dared not meet the Daffodils –
For fear their Yellow Gown
Would pierce me with a fashion
So foreign to my own –

I wished the Grass would hurry –
So – when 'twas time to see –
He'd be too tall, the tallest one
Could stretch – to look at me –

I could not bear the Bees should come,
I wished they'd stay away
In those dim countries where they go,
What word had they, for me?

They're here, though; not a creature failed –
No Blossom stayed away
In gentle deference to me –
The Queen of Calvary –

Each one salutes me, as he goes,
And I, my childish Plumes,
Lift, in bereaved acknowledgment
Of their unthinking Drums –

I had no time to Hate –
Because
The Grave would hinder Me –
And Life was not so
Ample I
Could finish – Enmity –

Nor had I time to Love –
But since
Some Industry must be –
The little Toil of Love –
I thought
Be large enough for Me –

Love – thou art high –
I cannot climb thee –
But, were it Two –
Who knows but we –
Taking turns – at the Chimborazo –
Ducal – at last – stand up by thee –

Love – thou art deep –
I cannot cross thee –
But, were there Two
Instead of One –
Rower, and Yacht – some sovereign Summer –
Who knows – but we'd reach the Sun?

Love – thou art Veiled –
A few – behold thee –
Smile – and alter – and prattle – and die –
Bliss – were an Oddity – without thee –
Nicknamed by God –
Eternity –

Love reckons by itself – alone –
"As large as I" – relate the Sun
To One who never felt it blaze –
Itself is all the like it has –

Love – is that later Thing than Death –
More previous – than Life –
Confirms it at its entrance – And
Usurps it – of itself –

Tastes Death – the first – to hand the sting
The Second – to its friend –
Disarms the little interval –
Deposits Him with God –

Then hovers – an inferior Guard –
Lest this Beloved Charge
Need – once in an Eternity –
A smaller than the Large –

Behold this little Bane –
The Boon of all alive –
As common as it is unknown
The name of it is Love –

To lack of it is Woe –
To own of it is Wound –
Not elsewhere – if in Paradise
Its Tantamount be found –

One Sister have I in our house,
And one, a hedge away.
There's only one recorded,
But both belong to me.

One came the road that I came –
And wore my last year's gown –
The other, as a bird her nest,
Builded our hearts among.

She did not sing as we did –
It was a different tune –
Herself to her a music
As Bumble bee of June.

Today is far from Childhood –
But up and down the hills
I held her hand the tighter –
Which shortened all the miles –

And still her hum
The years among,
Deceives the Butterfly;
Still in her Eye
The Violets lie
Mouldered this many May.

I spilt the dew –
But took the morn –
I chose this single star
From out the wide night's numbers –
Sue – forevermore!

139

I never hear the word "escape"
Without a quicker blood,
A sudden expectation,
A flying attitude!

I never hear of prisons broad
By soldiers battered down,
But I tug childish at my bars
Only to fail again!

140

"Why do I love" You, Sir?
Because –
The Wind does not require the Grass
To answer – Wherefore when He pass
She cannot keep Her place.

Because He knows – and
Do not You –
And We know not –
Enough for Us
The Wisdom it be so –

The Lightning – never asked an Eye
Wherefore it shut – when He was by –
Because He knows it cannot speak –
And reasons not contained –
– Of Talk –
There be – preferred by Daintier Folk –

The Sunrise – Sir – compelleth Me –
Because He's Sunrise – and I see –
Therefore – Then –
I love Thee –

141

Had this one Day not been,
Or could it cease to be
How smitten, how superfluous,
Were every other Day!

Lest Love should value less
What Loss would value more
Had it the stricken privilege,
It cherishes before.

The Love a Life can show Below
Is but a filament, I know,
Of that diviner thing
That faints upon the face of Noon –
And smites the Tinder in the Sun –
And hinders Gabriel's Wing –

'Tis this – in Music – hints and sways –
And far abroad on Summer days –
Distils uncertain pain –
'Tis this enamors in the East –
And tints the Transit in the West
With harrowing Iodine –

'Tis this – invites – appalls – endows –
Flits – glimmers – proves – dissolves –
Returns – suggests – convicts – enchants –
Then – flings in Paradise –

143

There came a Day at Summer's full,
Entirely for me –
I thought that such were for the Saints,
Where Resurrections – be –

The Sun, as common, went abroad,
The flowers, accustomed, blew,
As if no soul the solstice passed
That maketh all things new –

The time was scarce profaned, by speech –
The symbol of a word
Was needless, as at Sacrament,
The Wardrobe – of our Lord –

Each was to each The Sealed Church,
Permitted to commune this – time –
Lest we too awkward show
At Supper of the Lamb.

The Hours slid fast – as Hours will,
Clutched tight, by greedy hands –
So faces on two Decks, look back,
Bound to opposing lands –

And so when all the time had leaked,
Without external sound
Each bound the Other's Crucifix –
We gave no other Bond –

Sufficient troth, that we shall rise –
Deposed – at length, the Grave –
To that new Marriage,
Justified – through Calvaries of Love –

144

You left me – Sire – two Legacies –
A Legacy of Love
A Heavenly Father would suffice
Had He the offer of –

You left me Boundaries of Pain –
Capacious as the Sea –
Between Eternity and Time –
Your Consciousness – and Me –

I cautious, scanned my little life –
I winnowed what would fade
From what would last till Heads like mine
Should be a-dreaming laid.

I put the latter in a Barn –
The former, blew away.
I went one winter morning
And lo – my priceless Hay

Was not upon the "Scaffold" –
Was not upon the "Beam" –
And from a thriving Farmer –
A Cynic, I became.

Whether a Thief did it –
Whether it was the wind –
Whether Deity's guiltless –
My business is, to find!

So I begin to ransack!
How is it Hearts, with Thee?
Art thou within the little Barn
Love provided Thee?

It ceased to hurt me, though so slow
I could not feel the Anguish go –
But only knew by looking back –
That something – had benumbed the Track –

Nor when it altered, I could say,
For I had worn it, every day,
As constant as the Childish frock –
I hung upon the Peg, at night.

But not the Grief – that nestled close
As needles – ladies softly press
To Cushions Cheeks –
To keep their place –

Nor what consoled it, I could trace –
Except, whereas 'twas Wilderness –
It's better – almost Peace –

Her sweet Weight on my Heart a Night
Had scarcely deigned to lie –
When, stirring, for Belief's delight,
My Bride had slipped away –

If 'twas a Dream – made solid – just
The Heaven to confirm –
Or if Myself were dreamed of Her –
The power to presume –

With Him remain – who unto Me –
Gave – even as to All –
A Fiction superseding Faith –
By so much – as 'twas real –

148

Drowning is not so pitiful
As the attempt to rise.
Three times, 'tis said, a sinking man
Comes up to face the skies,
And then declines forever
To that abhorred abode,
Where hope and he part company –
For he is grasped of God.
The Maker's cordial visage,
However good to see,
Is shunned, we must admit it,
Like an adversity.

149

He was my host – he was my guest,
I never to this day
If I invited him could tell,
Or he invited me.

So infinite our intercourse
So intimate, indeed,
Analysis as capsule seemed
To keeper of the seed.

150

Of Course – I prayed –
And did God Care?
He cared as much as on the Air
A Bird – had stamped her foot –
And cried "Give Me" –
My Reason – Life –
I had not had – but for Yourself –
'Twere better Charity
To leave me in the Atom's Tomb –
Merry, and Nought, and gay, and numb –
Than this smart Misery.

My period had come for Prayer –
No other Art – would do –
My Tactics missed a rudiment –
Creator – Was it you?

God grows above – so those who pray
Horizons – must ascend –
And so I stepped upon the North
To see this Curious Friend –

His House was not – no sign had He –
By Chimney – nor by Door
Could I infer his Residence –
Vast Prairies of Air

Unbroken by a Settler –
Were all that I could see –
Infinitude – Had'st Thou no Face
That I might look on Thee?

The Silence condescended –
Creation stopped – for Me –
But awed beyond my errand –
I worshipped – did not "pray" –

All Circumstances are the Frame
In which His Face is set –
All Latitudes exist for His
Sufficient Continent –

The Light His Action, and the Dark
The Leisure of His Will –
In Him Existence serve or set
A Force illegible.

153

The look of thee, what is it like
Hast thou a hand or Foot
Or Mansion of Identity
And what is thy Pursuit?

Thy fellows are they realms or Themes
Hast thou Delight or Fear
Or Longing – and is that for us
Or values more severe?

Let change transfuse all other Traits
Enact all other Blame
But deign this least certificate –
That thou shalt be the same.

154

It was too late for Man –
But early, yet, for God –
Creation – impotent to help –
But Prayer – remained – Our Side –

How excellent the Heaven –
When Earth – cannot be had –
How hospitable – then – the face
Of our Old Neighbor – God –

Victory comes late –
And is held low to freezing lips –
Too rapt with frost
To take it –
How sweet it would have tasted –
Just a Drop –
Was God so economical?
His Table's spread too high for Us –
Unless We dine on tiptoe –
Crumbs – fit such little mouths –
Cherries – suit Robins –
The Eagle's Golden Breakfast strangles – Them –
God keep His Oath to Sparrows –
Who of little Love – know how to starve –

The Heaven vests for Each
In that small Deity
It craved the grace to worship
Some bashful Summer's Day –

Half shrinking from the Glory
It importuned to see
Till these faint Tabernacles drop
In full Eternity –

How imminent the Venture –
As one should sue a Star –
For His mean sake to leave the Row
And entertain Despair –

A Clemency so common –
We almost cease to fear –
Enabling the minutest –
And furthest – to adore –

Just as He spoke it from his Hands
This Edifice remain –
A Turret more, a Turret less
Dishonor his Design –

According as his skill prefer
It perish, or endure –
Content, soe'er, it ornament
His absent character.

158

The Moon upon her fluent Route
Defiant of a Road –
The Star's Etruscan Argument
Substantiate a God –

If Aims impel these Astral Ones
The ones allowed to know
Know that which makes them as forgot
As Dawn forgets them – now –

159
Escaping backward to perceive
The Sea upon our place –
Escaping forward, to confront
His glittering Embrace –

Retreating up, a Billow's height
Retreating blinded down
Our undermining feet to meet
Instructs to the Divine.

Just Once! Oh least Request!
Could Adamant refuse
So small a Grace
So scanty put,
Such agonizing terms?
Would not a God of Flint
Be conscious of a sigh
As down His Heaven dropt remote
"Just Once" Sweet Deity?

DEATH AND
RESURRECTION

Because I could not stop for Death –
He kindly stopped for me –
The Carriage held but just Ourselves –
And Immortality.

We slowly drove – He knew no haste
And I had put away
My labor and my leisure too,
For His Civility –

We passed the School, where Children strove
At Recess – in the Ring –
We passed the Fields of Gazing Grain –
We passed the Setting Sun –

Or rather – He passed Us –
The Dews drew quivering and chill –
For only Gossamer, my Gown –
My Tippet – only Tulle –

We paused before a House that seemed
A Swelling of the Ground –
The Roof was scarcely visible –
The Cornice – in the Ground –

Since then – 'tis Centuries – and yet
Feels shorter than the Day
I first surmised the Horses' Heads
Were toward Eternity –

I heard a Fly buzz – when I died –
The Stillness in the Room
Was like the Stillness in the Air –
Between the Heaves of Storm –

The Eyes around – had wrung them dry –
And Breaths were gathering firm
For that last Onset – when the King
Be witnessed – in the Room –

I willed my Keepsakes – Signed away
What portion of me be
Assignable – and then it was
There interposed a Fly –

With Blue – uncertain stumbling Buzz –
Between the light – and me –
And then the Windows failed – and then
I could not see to see –

Today or this noon
She dwelt so close
I almost touched her –
Tonight she lies
Past neighborhood
And bough and steeple,
Now past surmise.

That it will never come again
Is what makes life so sweet.
Believing what we don't believe
Does not exhilarate.

That if it be, it be at best
An ablative estate –
This instigates an appetite
Precisely opposite.

A throe upon the features –
A hurry in the breath –
An ecstasy of parting
Denominated "Death" –

An anguish at the mention
Which when to patience grown,
I've known permission given
To rejoin its own.

166

Departed – to the Judgment –
A Mighty Afternoon –
Great Clouds – like Ushers – leaning –
Creation – looking on –

The Flesh – Surrendered – Cancelled –
The Bodiless – begun –
Two Worlds – like Audiences – disperse –
And leave the Soul – alone –

All but Death, can be Adjusted –
Dynasties repaired –
Systems – settled in their Sockets –
Citadels – dissolved –

Wastes of Lives – resown with Colors
By Succeeding Springs –
Death – unto itself – Exception –
Is exempt from Change –

168

Death is a Dialogue between
The Spirit and the Dust.
"Dissolve" says Death – The Spirit "Sir
I have another Trust" –

Death doubts it – Argues from the Ground –
The Spirit turns away
Just laying off for evidence
An Overcoat of Clay.

Death is the supple Suitor
That wins at last –
It is a stealthy Wooing
Conducted first
By pallid innuendoes
And dim approach
But brave at last with Bugles
And a bisected Coach
It bears away in triumph
To Troth unknown
And Kindred as responsive
As Porcelain.

Good night, because we must,
How intricate the dust!
I would go, to know!
Oh incognito!
Saucy, Saucy Seraph
To elude me so!
Father! they won't tell me,
Won't you tell them to?

If any sink, assure that this, now standing –
Failed like Themselves – and conscious that it rose –
Grew by the Fact, and not the Understanding
How Weakness passed – or Force – arose –

Tell that the Worst, is easy in a Moment –
Dread, but the Whizzing, before the Ball –
When the Ball enters, enters Silence –
Dying – annuls the power to kill.

Wait till the Majesty of Death
Invests so mean a brow!
Almost a powdered Footman
Might dare to touch it now!

Wait till in Everlasting Robes
That Democrat is dressed,
Then prate about "Preferment" –
And "Station," and the rest!

Around this quiet Courtier
Obsequious Angels wait!
Full royal is his Retinue!
Full purple is his state!

A Lord, might dare to lift the Hat
To such a Modest Clay
Since that My Lord, "the Lord of Lords"
Receives unblushingly!

For Death – or rather
For the Things 'twould buy –
This – put away
Life's Opportunity –

The Things that Death will buy
Are Room –
Escape from Circumstances –
And a Name –

With Gifts of Life
How Death's Gifts may compare –
We know not –
For the Rates – lie Here –

That this should feel the need of Death
The same as those that lived
Is such a Feat of Irony
As never was – achieved –

Not satisfied to ape the Great
In his simplicity
The small must die, as well as He –
Oh the Audacity –

To disappear enhances –
The Man that runs away
Is tinctured for an instant
With Immortality

But yesterday a Vagrant –
Today in Memory lain
With superstitious value
We tamper with "Again"

But "Never" far as Honor
Withdraws the Worthless thing
And impotent to cherish
We hasten to adorn –

Of Death the sternest function
That just as we discern
The Excellence defies us –
Securest gathered then

The Fruit perverse to plucking,
But leaning to the Sight
With the ecstatic limit
Of unobtained Delight –

Because that you are going
And never coming back
And I, however absolute,
May overlook your Track –

Because that Death is final,
However first it be,
This instant be suspended
Above Mortality –

Significance that each has lived
The other to detect
Discovery not God himself
Could now annihilate

Eternity, Presumption
The instant I perceive
That you, who were Existence
Yourself forgot to live –

The "Life that is" will then have been
A thing I never knew –
As Paradise fictitious
Until the Realm of you –

The "Life that is to be," to me,
A Residence too plain
Unless in my Redeemer's Face
I recognize your own –

Of Immortality who doubts
He may exchange with me
Curtailed by your obscuring Face
Of everything but He –

Of Heaven and Hell I also yield
The Right to reprehend
To whoso would commute this Face
For his less priceless Friend.

If "God is Love" as he admits
We think that he must be
Because he is a "jealous God"
He tells us certainly

If "All is possible with" him
As he besides concedes
He will refund us finally
Our confiscated Gods –

177

'Twas my one Glory –
Let it be
Remembered
I was owned of Thee –

You'll find – it when you try to die –
The Easier to let go –
For recollecting such as went –
You could not spare – you know.

And though their places somewhat filled –
As did their Marble names
With Moss – they never grew so full –
You chose the newer names –

And when this World – sets further back –
As Dying – say it does –
The former love – distincter grows –
And supersedes the fresh –

And Thought of them – so fair invites –
It looks too tawdry Grace
To stay behind – with just the Toys
We bought – to ease their place –

Upon Concluded Lives
There's nothing cooler falls –
Than Life's sweet Calculations –
The mixing Bells and Palls –

Makes Lacerating Tune –
To Ears the Dying Side –
'Tis Coronal – and Funeral –
Saluting – in the Road –

Some, too fragile for winter winds
The thoughtful grave encloses –
Tenderly tucking them in from frost
Before their feet are cold.

Never the treasures in her nest
The cautious grave exposes,
Building where schoolboy dare not look,
And sportsman is not bold.

This covert have all the children
Early aged, and often cold,
Sparrows, unnoticed by the Father –
Lambs for whom time had not a fold.

On this long storm the Rainbow rose –
On this late Morn – the Sun –
The clouds – like listless Elephants –
Horizons – straggled down –

The Birds rose smiling, in their nests –
The gales – indeed – were done –
Alas, how heedless were the eyes –
On whom the summer shone!

The quiet nonchalance of death –
No Daybreak – can bestir –
The slow – Archangel's syllables
Must awaken *her*!

I read my sentence – steadily –
Reviewed it with my eyes,
To see that I made no mistake
In its extremest clause –
The Date, and manner, of the shame –
And then the Pious Form
That "God have mercy" on the Soul
The Jury voted Him –
I made my soul familiar – with her extremity –
That at the last, it should not be a novel Agony –
But she, and Death, acquainted –
Meet tranquilly, as friends –
Salute, and pass, without a Hint –
And there, the Matter ends –

183

The Fact that Earth is Heaven –
Whether Heaven is Heaven or not
If not an Affidavit
Of that specific Spot
Not only must confirm us
That it is not for us
But that it would affront us
To dwell in such a place –

Than Heaven more remote,
For Heaven is the root,
But these the flitted seed,
More flown indeed
Than ones that never were,
Or those that hide, and are.

What madness, by their side,
A vision to provide
Of future days
They cannot praise.

My soul, to find them, come,
They cannot call, they're dumb,
Nor prove, nor woo,
But that they have abode
Is absolute as God,
And instant, too.

"Heaven" – is what I cannot reach!
The Apple on the Tree –
Provided it do hopeless – hang –
That – "Heaven" is – to Me!

The Color, on the Cruising Cloud –
The interdicted Land –
Behind the Hill – the House behind –
There – Paradise – is found!

Her teasing Purples – Afternoons –
The credulous – decoy –
Enamored – of the Conjuror –
That spurned us – Yesterday!

What is – "Paradise" –
Who live there –
Are they "Farmers" –
Do they "hoe" –
Do they know that this is "Amherst" –
And that I – am coming – too –

Do they wear "new shoes" – in "Eden" –
Is it always pleasant – there –
Won't they scold us – when we're homesick –
Or tell God – how cross we are –

You are sure there's such a person
As "a Father" – in the sky –
So if I get lost – there – ever –
Or do what the Nurse calls "die" –
I shan't walk the "Jasper" – barefoot –
Ransomed folks – won't laugh at me –
Maybe – "Eden" a'n't so lonesome
As New England used to be!

Paradise is of the option.
Whosoever will
Own in Eden notwithstanding
Adam and Repeal.

Lift it – with the Feathers
Not alone we fly –
Launch it – the aquatic
Not the only sea –
Advocate the Azure
To the lower Eyes –
He has obligation
Who has Paradise –

The Road to Paradise is plain,
And holds scarce one.
Not that it is not firm
But we presume
A Dimpled Road
Is more preferred.
The Belles of Paradise are few –
Not me – nor you –
But unsuspected things –
Mines have no Wings.

Their Height in Heaven comforts not –
Their Glory – nought to me –
'Twas best imperfect – as it was –
I'm finite – I can't see –

The House of Supposition –
The Glimmering Frontier that
Skirts the Acres of Perhaps –
To Me – shows insecure –

The Wealth I had – contented me –
If 'twas a meaner size –
Then I had counted it until
It pleased my narrow Eyes –

Better than larger values –
That show however true –
This timid life of Evidence
Keeps pleading – "I don't know."

Conscious am I in my Chamber,
Of a shapeless friend –
He doth not attest by Posture –
Nor Confirm – by Word –

Neither Place – need I present Him –
Fitter Courtesy
Hospitable intuition
Of His Company –

Presence – is His furthest license –
Neither He to Me
Nor Myself to Him – by Accent –
Forfeit Probity –

Weariness of Him, were quainter
Than Monotony
Knew a Particle – of Space's
Vast Society –

Neither if He visit Other –
Do He dwell – or Nay – know I –
But Instinct esteem Him
Immortality –

192

It is an honorable Thought
And makes One lift One's Hat
As One met sudden Gentlefolk
Upon a daily Street

That We've immortal Place
Though Pyramids decay
And Kingdoms, like the Orchard
Flit Russetly away

If my Bark sink
'Tis to another sea –
Mortality's Ground Floor
Is Immortality –

This World is not Conclusion.
A Species stands beyond –
Invisible, as Music –
But positive, as Sound –
It beckons, and it baffles –
Philosophy – don't know –
And through a Riddle, at the last –
Sagacity, must go –
To guess it, puzzles scholars –
To gain it, Men have borne
Contempt of Generations
And Crucifixion, shown –
Faith slips – and laughs, and rallies –
Blushes, if any see –
Plucks at a twig of Evidence –
And asks a Vane, the way –
Much Gesture, from the Pulpit –
Strong Hallelujahs roll –
Narcotics cannot still the Tooth
That nibbles at the soul –

He scanned it – staggered –
Dropped the Loop
To Past or Period –
Caught helpless at a sense as if
His Mind were going blind –

Groped up, to see if God was there –
Groped backward at Himself
Caressed a Trigger absently
And wandered out of Life.

Somewhere upon the general Earth
Itself exist Today –
The Magic passive but extant
That consecrated me –

Indifferent Seasons doubtless play
Where I for right to be –
Would pay each Atom that I am
But Immortality –

Reserving that but just to prove
Another Date of Thee –
Oh God of Width, do not for us
Curtail Eternity!

Those not live yet
Who doubt to live again –
"Again" is of a twice
But this – is one –
The Ship beneath the Draw
Aground – is he?
Death – so – the Hyphen of the Sea –
Deep is the Schedule
Of the Disk to be –
Costumeless Consciousness –
That is he –

Who abdicated Ambush
And went the way of Dusk,
And now against his subtle Name
There stands an Asterisk
As confident of him as we –
Impregnable we are –
The whole of Immortality
Secreted in a Star.

My life closed twice before its close –
It yet remains to see
If Immortality unveil
A third event to me

So huge, so hopeless to conceive
As these that twice befell.
Parting is all we know of heaven,
And all we need of hell.

Forever – is composed of Nows –
'Tis not a different time –
Except for Infiniteness –
And Latitude of Home –

From this – experienced Here –
Remove the Dates – to These –
Let Months dissolve in further Months –
And Years – exhale in Years –

Without Debate – or Pause –
Or Celebrated Days –
No different Our Years would be
From Anno Domini's –

As if the Sea should part
And show a further Sea –
And that – a further – and the Three
But a presumption be –

Of Periods of Seas –
Unvisited of Shores –
Themselves the Verge of Seas to be –
Eternity – is Those –

The Blunder is in estimate.
Eternity is there
We say, as of a Station –
Meanwhile he is so near

He joins me in my Ramble –
Divides abode with me –
No Friend have I that so persists
As this Eternity.

Exultation is the going
Of an inland soul to sea,
Past the houses – past the headlands –
Into deep Eternity –

Bred as we, among the mountains,
Can the sailor understand
The divine intoxication
Of the first league out from land?

A Wife – at Daybreak I shall be –
Sunrise – Hast thou a Flag for me?
At Midnight, I am but a Maid,
How short it takes to make a Bride –
Then – Midnight, I have passed from thee
Unto the East, and Victory –

Midnight – Good Night! I hear them call,
The Angels bustle in the Hall –
Softly my Future climbs the Stair,
I fumble at my Childhood's prayer
So soon to be a Child no more –
Eternity, I'm coming – Sir,
Savior – I've seen the face – before!

Behind Me – dips Eternity –
Before Me – Immortality –
Myself – the Term between –
Death but the Drift of Eastern Gray,
Dissolving into Dawn away,
Before the West begin –

'Tis Kingdoms – afterward – they say –
In perfect – pauseless Monarchy –
Whose Prince – is Son of None –
Himself – His Dateless Dynasty –
Himself – Himself diversify –
In Duplicate divine –

'Tis Miracle before Me – then –
'Tis Miracle behind – between –
A Crescent in the Sea –
With Midnight to the North of Her –
And Midnight to the South of Her –
And Maelstrom – in the Sky –

206

Two Lengths has every Day –
Its absolute extent
And Area superior
By Hope or Horror lent –

Eternity will be
Velocity or Pause
At Fundamental Signals
From Fundamental Laws.

To die is not to go –
On Doom's consummate Chart
No Territory new is staked –
Remain thou as thou art.

207

The Infinite a sudden Guest
Has been assumed to be –
But how can that stupendous come
Which never went away?

INDEX OF FIRST LINES

A Bird came down the Walk 104

A Burdock – clawed my Gown 165

A chilly Peace infests the Grass 151

A feather from the Whippoorwill 133

A little Dog that wags his tail 95

A little East of Jordan 83

A little Madness in the Spring 144

A little Snow was here and there 77

A long – long Sleep – A famous – Sleep 85

A Moth the hue of this 145

A nearness to Tremendousness 62

A Prison gets to be a friend 88

A prompt – executive Bird is the Jay 115

A Rat surrendered here 98

A slash of Blue 164

A Spider sewed at Night 124

A throe upon the features 206

A wife – at Daybreak I shall be 246

A Wind that rose 155

A winged spark doth soar about 122

A Word dropped careless on a Page 31

A word is dead 30

Abraham to kill him 78

Afraid! Of whom am I afraid? 48

Again – his voice is at the door 68

All but Death, can be Adjusted 208
All Circumstances are the Frame 189
All overgrown by cunning moss 81
All the letters I can write 65
An Antiquated Tree 117
As if the Sea should part 243
As the Starved Maelstrom laps the Navies 100
At Half past Three, a single Bird 110
Because I could not stop for Death 201
Because that you are going 217
Bee! I'm expecting you!.. 118
Bees are Black, with Gilt Surcingles.. 131
Behind Me – dips Eternity 247
Behold this little Bane 172
Bring me the sunset in a cup.. 135
Civilization – spurns – the Leopard!.. 96
Conjecturing a Climate.. 136
Conscious am I in my Chamber 233
Could mortal lip divine.. 32
Death is a Dialogue between 209
Death is the supple Suitor.. 210
Delight – becomes pictorial 39
Departed – to the Judgment 207
Don't put up my Thread and Needle 51
Drab Habitation of Whom? 75
Drowning is not so pitiful.. 185
Each Life Converges to some Centre 58

Escaping backward to perceive.. 196

Exultation is the going.. 245

Flowers – Well – if anybody.. 163

For Death – or rather 214

Forever – is composed of Nows 242

From Cocoon forth a Butterfly.. 137

Good night, because we must 211

Had this one Day not been 177

He found my Being – set it up 44

He scanned it – staggered.. 237

He was my host – he was my guest 186

"Heaven" – is what I cannot reach! 227

Her final Summer was it 90

Her sweet Weight on my Heart a Night 184

His Feet are shod with Gauze 129

His little Hearse like Figure 132

His Mansion in the Pool 126

How lonesome the Wind must feel Nights 147

How soft a Caterpillar steps 121

I cannot live with You 53

I cautious, scanned my little life 182

I dreaded that first Robin, so 166

I dwell in Possibility.. 41

I had no time to Hate 168

I heard a Fly buzz – when I died 203

I never hear the word "escape".. 175

I read my sentence – steadily 224

I reckon – when I count at all   26

I should not dare to leave my friend   82

I started Early – Took my Dog..   45

I tie my Hat – I crease my Shawl   59

I would not paint – a picture..   20

I Years had been from Home   91

I'm Nobody! Who are you? 127

If any sink, assure that this, now standing 212

If I should cease to bring a Rose 143

If my Bark sink 235

It ceased to hurt me, though so slow.. 183

It is an honorable Thought 234

It makes no difference abroad 158

It troubled me as once I was   43

It was a quiet seeming Day 148

It was too late for Man 191

It would have starved a Gnat   49

Just as He spoke it from his hands 194

Just Once! Oh least Request!.. 197

Lift it – with the Feathers.. 230

Like Brooms of Steel.. 156

Like Trains of Cars on Tracks of Plush.. 130

Love – is that later Thing than Death 171

Love reckons by itself – alone .. .. – 170

Love – thou art high 169

Make me a picture of the sun   38

March is the Month of Expectation 146

Me from Myself – to banish   42

Most she touched me by her muteness 114

My life closed twice before its close 241

My period had come for Prayer 188

"Nature" is what we see 139

No Brigadier throughout the year 116

Of Course – I prayed.. 187

On this long storm the Rainbow rose 223

One Joy of so much anguish 112

One of the ones that Midas touched 102

One Sister have I in our house 173

Pain – has an Element of Blank..   61

Papa above!   93

Paradise is of the option 229

She dealt her pretty words like Blades   23

She dwelleth in the Ground   56

She sights a Bird – she chuckles   94

She staked her Feathers – Gained an Arc 111

So much Summer 159

Some things that fly there be 142

Some, too fragile for winter winds 222

Somewhere upon the general Earth 238

Speech is one symptom of Affection   33

Struck was I, not yet by Lightning   66

Summer begins to have the look 152

Summer has two Beginnings 149

Surgeons must be very careful   37

Tell all the Truth but tell it slant   18
Than Heaven more remote   226
That it will never come again   205
That this should feel the need of Death   215
The Bat is dun, with wrinkled Wings   120
The Bird her punctual music brings..   113
The Birds begun at Four o'clock   108
The Blunder is in estimate   244
The Butterfly in honored Dust..   119
The butterfly obtains   28
The Drop, that wrestles in the Sea   80
The Fact that Earth is Heaven   225
The farthest Thunder that I heard   154
The Gentian has a parched Corolla   150
The Heaven vests for Each   193
The Infinite a sudden Guest   248
The Judge is like the Owl   101
The long sigh of the Frog..   128
The look of thee, what is it like   190
The Love a Life can show Below   178
The Martyr Poets – did not tell   25
The Moon upon her fluent Route   195
The Murmur of a Bee   141
The nearest Dream recedes – unrealized   64
The Poets light but Lamps   27
The Rat is the concisest Tenant   99
The Road to Paradise is Plain   231

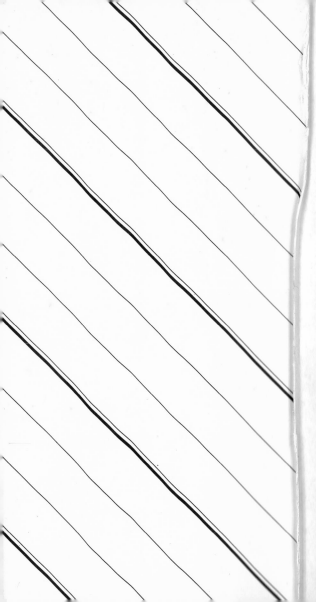

The Robin for the Crumb 105
The Spider as an Artist.. 125
The Spider holds a Silver Ball 123
The Sun kept stooping – stooping – low! 140
The Sweets of Pillage, can be known 87
The Trees like Tassels – hit – and swung.. 160
Their Height in Heaven comforts not 232
There came a Day at Summer's full 179
There is a solitude of space 76
These are the Nights that Beetles love 134
These the days when Birds come back 162
They called me to the Window, for 52
They shut me up in Prose.. 50
This is my letter to the World 17
This was a Poet – It is That 22
This World is not Conclusion 236
Those fair – fictitious People 35
Those not live yet.. 239
To be alive – is Power 57
To disappear enhances 216
To hear an Oriole sing 107
To interrupt His Yellow Plan 157
To pile like Thunder to its close 24
To see the Summer Sky 19
To tell the Beauty would decrease 34
Today or this noon 204
'Twas my one Glory.. 219

'Twas such a little – little boat 63
Two Lengths has every Day.. 248
Unto my Books – So good to turn.. 47
Upon Concluded Lives 221
Upon his Saddle sprung a Bird 106
Victory comes late   192
Wait till the Majesty of Death 213
We – Bee and I – live by the quaffing 29
We talked as Girls do 86
What is – "Paradise".. 228
What we see we know somewhat 79
When I was small, a Woman died.. 84
Who abdicated Ambush 240
Who occupies this House? 73
"Why do I love" You, Sir? .. .. ·. 176
With sweetness unabated.. 153
Within my Garden, rides a Bird 97
You left me – Sire – two Legacies 181
You'll find – it when you try to die 220
Your thoughts don't have words every day 40